Ancient China for Kids

A Captivating Guide to Ancient Chinese History, from the Shang Dynasty to the Fall of the Han Dynasty

© Copyright 2021

All Rights Reserved. No part of this book may be reproduced in any form without permission in writing from the author. Reviewers may quote brief passages in reviews.

Disclaimer: No part of this publication may be reproduced or transmitted in any form or by any means, mechanical or electronic, including photocopying or recording, or by any information storage and retrieval system, or transmitted by email without permission in writing from the publisher.

While all attempts have been made to verify the information provided in this publication, neither the author nor the publisher assumes any responsibility for errors, omissions or contrary interpretations of the subject matter herein.

This book is for entertainment purposes only. The views expressed are those of the author alone, and should not be taken as expert instruction or commands. The reader is responsible for his or her own actions.

Adherence to all applicable laws and regulations, including international, federal, state and local laws governing professional licensing, business practices, advertising and all other aspects of doing business in the US, Canada, UK or any other jurisdiction is the sole responsibility of the purchaser or reader.

Neither the author nor the publisher assumes any responsibility or liability whatsoever on the behalf of the purchaser or reader of these materials. Any perceived slight of any individual or organization is purely unintentional.

Table of Contents

Introduction..1

Chapter 1: The First Settlements...2

Chapter 2: The Mythical Xia Dynasty and Yu, The Great 9

Chapter 3: The Shang Dynasty: China's Bronze Age Wonder..............13

Chapter 4: The Zhou Dynasty...18

Chapter 5: The Qin Dynasty...23

Chapter 6: The Han Dynasty..28

Chapter 7: Inventions, Arts and Trade...33

Chapter 8: The Armies of Ancient China.....................................47

Chapter 9: Chinese Philosophy and Religions..............................57

Chapter 10: Customs and Festivities..62

Bibliography..75

INTRODUCTION

Heroes, evil emperors, legends of men who fought against nine-headed snakes, and sorcerers that could tell the future are all here in this book. So why should you read this book?

History is fascinating. It teaches us not to make the same mistakes as those that came before us.

It shows us the power of the people who lived long ago and inspires us to be better.

This book is an in-depth look at the great history of Ancient China. From the Great Wall of China to inventing paper, Ancient China has been an important part of our world's development.

By picking up this book, you are giving yourself the gift of reading information that is not only interesting but real, too. How cool is that!

Chapter 1: The First Settlements

The Yellow River Valley

Imagine a time without Nintendo Switch and Pokémon. I know it is hard, or maybe even impossible to do, but thousands of years ago, people lived without all the fun and convenient things we have that make our lives so easy today. People lived off the land because it was all they had. They made their pottery, clothes, homes, and they hunted for food themselves. Most of us have watched some survival shows on TV, but let me tell you, these people were the original real survivors.

The Yellow River Valley was where ancient Chinese civilizations started. It is often called "Mother River" because civilizations were born here, two in particular: the Yangshao and Longshan cultures. The river has played an important part in Ancient China. We will learn more about all the people who lived in the areas around the river. It was their home, and it gave them food, water, and materials.

The Yangshao Culture

During the final stage of the stone age, a small civilization started along the Yellow River Valley called the *Yangshao Culture*. The Yangshao Culture dated from 5000 BCE to 3000 BCE; now, that is quite some time ago! Let's read about how they lived.

Food

The Yangshao Culture couldn't just push a few buttons on their phones and have an UberEATS driver bring them their favorite meals. When they were hungry, they needed to search for their food. They mostly lived on millet and rice, and enjoyed the rich river soil. However, when the earth became overused, they packed up their belongings and moved to a new spot down the river. Can you imagine having to pack up all your belongings today just to move a few meters down the street? That was a way of life for the Yangshao Culture. They kept pigs and dogs, and on occasion, cows, sheep, and goats. If they wanted to eat meat instead of millet and rice, they caught fish from the river. They used stone tools to catch fish.

Houses

The Yangshao Culture used clay, mud, poles made from trees, and millet stalks to build their houses. They built a pen outside for animals. The houses were simple, but it was a safe place for people to rest after a long day after working outside.

Crafts

The Yangshao culture made pottery, and they decorated it with fine white, red, and black paint. They loved painting their faces, animals, and shapes on their pottery. We can still see some of their pottery in Chinese museums today.

They also made silk and wove hemp. This was used to make loincloths for the men. The woman wore a cloth around their bodies.

Now before we jump into the Longshan culture, *it is joke time!*

Why is a History book like a fruit cake? It is full of dates.

Dates! Get it? Come on, that's funny!

The Longshan Culture

After the Yangshao culture, the Longshan culture existed from about 3000 BCE. They are sometimes called the Black Pottery Culture. Can you guess why? Yes, they mastered black pottery making - but more about that later. They lived in the middle and lower Yellow River valley areas. Let's learn more about them.

Yangshao map Credit: Kanguole
https://commons.wikimedia.org/wiki/File:Yangshao_map.svg

Food

They enjoyed millet, rice, and wheat, and their favorite source of meat was pigs. They started herding animals, and they had chickens, pigs, dogs - and sometimes cattle. The Longshan culture loved growing plants and crops, and they used the river's fertile soil very well. They had a much more exciting diet than the Yangshao culture because they were smart about using the land.

Crafts

Yangshao artifacts
https://www.flickr.com/photos/101561334@N08/10339484864/

They produced some silk by keeping silkworms, but they are most remembered for their black pottery. Their pottery was beautiful and can still be seen today. Not all their pottery was black. At times they also made grey and white pottery. They made cooking pots and egg shelling pots. What are egg shelling pots, you might ask? If you guessed that they are pots used for shelling eggs, then you are right!

Tongue twister challenge! Can you say this three times fast without getting your tongue twisted? *The Longshan culture made egg shelling pots to shell eggs.* Could you do it?

Longshan weapons
https://commons.wikimedia.org/wiki/File:Longshan_Culture_Stone_Weapons.jpg

Houses

The Longshan culture lived in houses made the same way as the Yangshao culture. In fact, these two cultures lived very much the same way. The biggest difference was that the Longshan culture was much more focused on growing crops, and their pottery skills were better. The Longshan culture also made more tools, especially for planting rice and grinding wheat. Having more tools made it easier for them to plant their seeds better. That resulted in better crops and happier people with full bellies.

What problems did these cultures face?

Both cultures were lucky to live off a river as rich and fertile as the Yellow River, but this had a downside. Jealous tribes would often come to take what wasn't theirs. They would attack the cultures, stealing their animals, food, and tools. *Now that's just mean.* So, the people had to learn to stand together and fight back against these bullying tribes. After all, many people are much more powerful than one. This was hard to get used to since everyone wanted to take charge. After some time and more annoying tribe attacks, it became clear that the cultures needed a leader, someone who told, while the others followed. That became the first rise of the ancient Chinese civilization's single tribe leader. The leader was a shaman-chief that led the people through hardships. When he died, the shaman-chief was surrounded by dragon and tiger figures that the people had made from clamshells.

The tiger and dragon figures were meant to protect the shaman-chief in the afterlife. Who would bother you if you had tigers and dragons by your side? Many decades later, these dragon and tiger figures were found in a small area that had been a Yangshao village.

Another uncontrollable problem they faced was floods. Flooding was a big problem for the cultures because it meant losing their homes and crops and often their belongings. Once again, this was just a way of life for the people of the Yangshao and Longshan cultures. Nature gave, and sometimes Nature took. All they could do was save what they could and start again with what they had. After a flood, they would take what could still be used and move to a new area along the river. Luckily for them, the river was always a reliable friend.

What can we learn from them?

The Yangshao and Longshan cultures were creative, hardworking, and tough. They faced lots of challenges, but they never gave up. Just like them, we also face challenges in our lives at times. So, stay strong, and never give up because you are a true survivor like the Yangshao and Longshan cultures!

Chapter 2: The Mythical Xia Dynasty and Yu, The Great

The First Dynasty

Now we move on to something so mythical that it is only spoken about in legends. In 2070 BCE, The Xia Dynasty was founded by Yu the Great, a legendary ruler of ancient China. It was the first dynasty in traditional Chinese history. Before the Western Zhou dynasty (which was more than 1000 years later), there was no information about the Xia dynasty. So people started to believe that it was just a mystical legend, and that Yu was changed into human form for our history.

Yu the Great
https://en.wikipedia.org/wiki/Yu_the_Great#/media/File:King_Yu_of_Xia.jpg

Yu, the Great

Before the Xia dynasty, it was a time called The Three Sovereigns and Five Emperors. Three demigods (half-god, half-human) ruled over the lands, with five emperors being their human helpers. One of the five emperors who helped the demigods was called Emperor Zhuanxu. He had a son, Gun, who had another son, Yu. Emperor Zhuanxu's grandson would grow up to be Yu, the Great.

Yu grew up in the mountains surrounding the yellow river. The river was constantly flooding, and people were tired of the damage. One of the five emperors asked Yu's father to find the solution to this problem. Yu's father tried his best to solve this problem for nine long years, but the flooding continued. Finally, he built dams to gather the water, but one of his dams collapsed, and people got hurt. The emperor was furious and imprisoned Yu's father for his failure.

The river flooding was now Yu's problem to fix. Instead of being scared or angry because of what happened to his dad, Yu was determined to learn from his father's mistakes. He organized tribes from all over the region to build a system that would flow the water out to sea. Yu became a confident builder over the years and started building amazing dams and canals all over China. He gave the tribes a new purpose. Yu was very popular among the tribes because he would work - and even eat and sleep - with them. This made them love him and motivated them to give him their best. He was a great leader because he saw himself as one of the people.

Yu's projects to improve the land took thirteen years to complete. During that time, the tribes adored him - even worshipped him. He was the one they had been waiting for.

There are stories about Yu's bravery. It is said that Yu defeated a nine-headed snake with the help of a yellow dragon and a black turtle. Now that is a fierce battle! It's believed that he did so much for the land and the people that the gods offered him special help. He traveled through China while sitting on the back of a 10,000-year-old turtle. I hope it was a fast turtle. Some believe that the river gods gave him maps of rivers, and he cleared entire channels in the mountains with his mighty ax.

Yu's hard work was so excellent that he was seen as a superhuman. He was a very dedicated builder. For thirteen years, he worked across the land. He didn't return to his home to his wife once during that time. He passed his front door three times in the thirteen years, but he never went in. He didn't even turn back when his young son saw him for the first time and called out his name. He dug mud day after day, year after year, until the job was done. He was unstoppable.

Temple of Yu The Great
https://commons.wikimedia.org/wiki/File:Temple_of_Yu_the_Great_in_Shaoxing,_Zhejiang,_China.jpg

Yu Becomes Emperor Yu

One of the five emperors, Emperor Shun, was amazed by the wonderful structures that Yu had built and how the tribes adored him. He was so impressed that he offered to pass the throne to Yu even though he had a son who was supposed to take over the throne. At first, Yu refused to take the throne, but with the community behind him, he changed his mind and took his place as *Emperor Yu* when he was 33 years old. That was when the Xia dynasty was born.

Yu was a very popular and good emperor, and he took great care of his people. Yu ruled for 45 years and passed the throne to his son, Qi, when he died while hunting. Yu was such a legendary figure that he is one of the few Chinese leaders that carry the title "Great."

The End of The Xia Dynasty

After Yu died, the throne was passed from emperor to emperor. The dynasty started to weaken until it was ruled by Emperor Jie, in 1600 BCE, who was mean and hard on the people. Emperor Jie was soon overthrown by King Tang, who was the first king of the Shang Dynasty.

Riddle challenge! Can you solve this riddle?
It is a place with lots of history
It includes the Ming Dynasty
Shanghai is the largest city
Art and pottery are found a plenty
What country is it?

Answer: *China*

Chapter 3: The Shang Dynasty: China's Bronze Age Wonder

The Almighty Emperor Tang

Emperor Tang was the Chinese emperor who overthrew the horrible Emperor Jie. Emperor Tang founded the Shang Dynasty in 1600 BCE.

It is said that Tang was the great-grandson of the mythical sage-king, Huangdi, the Yellow Emperor. Legends tell us that Tang read about the evil ruler Jie on the shell of a tortoise, and he knew he had to step up and claim the dynasty.

Tang was a great and generous leader to his people who always offered whatever he could to make sure they were happy. It is said that a drought made his people unhappy because all of their crops died. Determined to end the drought at any cost, Tang offered himself to the heavens, and it started to rain heavily, saving the people and their leader. In drawings of Tang, he is shown as at least 9 feet tall, with a white face and whiskers. He had a very pointed head and arms that were six-jointed. What a magnificent emperor!

The Birth of the Bronze Age

As the Shang Dynasty continued to strengthen, the Chinese Bronze Age began around 1700 BCE along the banks of the Yellow River. Although the Shang kings who came after Tang ruled areas much larger than that, their attention stayed on the yellow river and the development of this wonderful Bronze Age.

Weapons and Tools

The Bronze Age was a very exciting time when men learned how to make bronze weapons and tools by mining and smelting copper. Bronze is much harder and lasts longer than copper, so soon, people were learning how to make all of their tools and weapons out of Bronze. To make weapons and tools, the people needed skilled artisans. They would develop the best weapons and tools they could by learning and experimenting with what the Yellow River gave them.

Before the Bronze Age started, people made their tools using stone, and they hunted with spears. With the Bronze Age, they had the chance to learn how to farm to have more food to feed others who offered them a service. They could get the help of miners, smiths, weavers, potters, and builders who lived in the small towns by feeding them. Years after the Shang Dynasty ended, ruins of old music instruments were found. This tells us that the Shang people were curious about music, and they made many different instruments using copper.

Food

We often believe that they drank tea and ate rice, but this isn't true. Rice and tea came from the south, and the Yellow River didn't care much for either until hundreds of years later. The people of the Bronze Age enjoyed eating cereals, bread, and cakes made of millet and barley. They drank beer. Those who could afford it added meat and wine to their meals.

The First Chinese Scripts

The people were not only farming and making bronze tools and weapons, but they also started writing. Using oracle bones made of animal bones or parts of a turtle's shell, people started engraving, which was the earliest form of Chinese writing. The Shang people wrote on these oracle bones to talk to their ancestors. They believed their ancestors had the power to give them fortune and keep disasters away from them. They also thought that their ancestors gave them guidance that would make them successful and keep them healthy. The sky also guided the people as they believed their ancestors hid messages within the stars, so they started with the Shang calendar.

Early Chinese writing (Shang Dynasty oracle bones)
https://www.flickr.com/photos/101561334@N08/9830601816

The Bronze Age Chinese had powerful ideas about what made a strong leader, and they believed the king had to have the best relationship with his ancestors. Therefore, those ancestors controlled his kingdom's success. Kings were encouraged to communicate with their ancestors, often using oracle bones. To get an answer from the ancestors, a priest held a hot rod to the bone until it cracked, and then he interpreted the pattern of the cracks for the ancestors' answers.

Bronze coins

Before the time of the Shang Dynasty, people traded what they needed using shell money. Yes, shells were used as money. Can you imagine buying your favorite candy bar with a handful of shells today? When the Bronze Age came, the people started making bronze coins for trading. This was the beginning of using coins as money, something that we are still using today.

Early Chinese currency (Shang cowrie coins)
https://commons.wikimedia.org/wiki/File:005_Xia_or_Shang_Bone_Cowrie_Money.jpg

The Shang Kings' Duties

The king's responsibility was to keep the city safe, so the Shang kings spent most of their time riding around their cities with their nobles and knights to hunt and fight wars. The kings appointed people who would oversee the farmers since they were peasants who belonged to the land.

The Shang people believed that the sun and rain gods controlled the harvest. Therefore, it was the king's duty to keep them happy. If the rain and sun gods gave the Shang Dynasty good harvests, they would show their thanks by placing wine and cereal in specially made bronze bowls and heat them over a fire at an altar.

The End of the Shang Dynasty

Around the year 1046 BCE, the Shang Dynasty was ruled by an evil and cruel king, King Di Xin, who didn't care for his people. The Shang people were unhappy. Conquerors from Zhou wanted to defeat the evil king because heaven told them the horrible king's ruling had to end.

A powerful leader of the Zhou, a state of the Shang Dynasty, named Wen Wang knew it would be up to him to make the suffering stop. He had to take over from the evil king. It took many years, but finally, his son, Wu Wang, led an army across the Yellow River and defeated the evil King Di Xin. King Wu established a new dynasty known as the Zhou Dynasty.

The end of King Di Xin's reign would become a message to all emperors for years to come. Be good to your people, Kings, or a better king will step in and take your place.

Chapter 4: The Zhou Dynasty

The Longest Dynasty

The Zhou Dynasty was founded in 1046, and it became the longest dynasty in the history of Chinese dynasties, stretching to 256 BCE. It was not just the longest dynasty but also the most important when it comes to Chinese culture. The Zhou Dynasty was divided into two periods. Western Zhuo lasted from 1046 to 771 BCE, and Eastern Zhou lasted from 771 to 256 BCE.

The Zhou Dynasty believed in the king's ruling above all else, which led to them inventing the Mandate of Heaven. The Mandate of Heaven stated that the heavens sent the kings and that there could be only one king to rule China, one king to rule over all the nobles. It would be used to justify the rule of one emperor ever since.

The Iron Age

The Zhou people were using bronze in better ways than ever before. They were fantastic at smelting metals at high temperatures and hammering them until they made perfect tools and weapons. At the end of the Shang Dynasty, bronze was still mostly used, but people started using iron as the Zhou Dynasty grew and developed. For example, they used meteoric iron, iron from meteors that crashed into Earth very long ago. Now that is out of this world!

The Western Zhou

The first half of the Zhou Dynasty was the Western Zhou. The people were masters of weapon making. They made many weapons, including swords, spears, bows, war chariots, and shields for defending themselves in battle. Their most impressive weapon was a dagger axe. It was the weapon every soldier carried. These weapons made it possible for them to protect their land and their people against tribal attacks. The people could farm happily, knowing that their crops will be protected.

Western Zhou bronze fittings (tigers) Credit: Mary Harrsch
tps://www.flickr.com/photos/mharrsch/19912564642/in/photostream/

The early years of Western Zhou were very successful, with the people growing in knowledge and power. However, this only lasted about 75 years. The dynasty created a system of order that would help the king reign over the growing land. It was known

as the Fengjian policy, and the power ran in this order:
- King
- Nobles (people with noble birth)
- Gentries (Upper-class people)
- Merchants (people who sold or traded goods)
- Laborers (workers)
- Peasants (people of low status)

Every noble formed his own little state with its own legal system, tax code, money, and army. However, every state still had to respect the king's ruling. They had to pay taxes to the king and give him their soldiers whenever he asked. The Fengjian policy was very successful, and the dynasty flourished. This was one of the few times in the history of Ancient China that the upper and lower classes worked together for the greater common good. But, unfortunately, the peaceful time could not last. The king was slowly losing control over the people because they wanted to be free to do as they please without a king's ruling. It got worse and worse until, in 771 BCE, the Zhou were forced out of the Yellow River valley, and King You of Zhou was killed. The people had taken control of the land.

The Eastern Zhou

Eastern Zhou bronze yi and pan Credit: Gary Todd
https://upload.wikimedia.org/wikipedia/commons/c/c0/Eastern_Zhou_Bronze_Yi_%26_Pan.jpg

After the fall of Western Zhou, it was the beginning of the Eastern Zhou. This era lasted 515 years, and 25 kings in that time ruled the dynasty in that time. The Eastern Zhou was divided into two periods. The first half of the dynasty was called the Spring and Autumn

Period. The second half of the Eastern Zhou Dynasty was called the Warring States period.

The Spring and Autumn Period

When the Eastern Zhou Dynasty started, there was a period called the Spring and Autumn Period. Although the name sounds quite peaceful and friendly, it was a time full of battles and conflict. The people were fighting against the idea of one king for all. Instead, they wanted the states of the dynasty to have their own power.

After the capital of Zhengzhou was attacked by a group of non-Chinese tribals, the Zhou moved the capital east so that it would be close to the people who would support it. However, they waited too long. By that time, it was already too late for the Zhou. There were four mighty states known as Qin, Jin, Qi, and Chu. They already started fighting together against the one king rule.

Along with the battles and the fighting, this period was a great time for music, poetry, and philosophy in Ancient China's history. This was the time of Confucius, Sun Tzu, and Lao Tzu and their teachings.

Eastern Zhou royal chariot pit Credit: Gary Todd
https://commons.wikimedia.org/wiki/File:Eastern_Zhou_Royal_Chariot_Pit._Luoyang_17.jpg

The Warring States Period

This period was not a peaceful time at all. In fact, it was filled with battles over dominance. However, in the end, it was the Qin state that won, and it became the first Chinese state. The other state rulers looked up to the Qin state and followed its example. They all declared themselves king of their own states, ending the one king rule. With each state ruled by its own leader, the states improved in family, philosophy, and the arts.

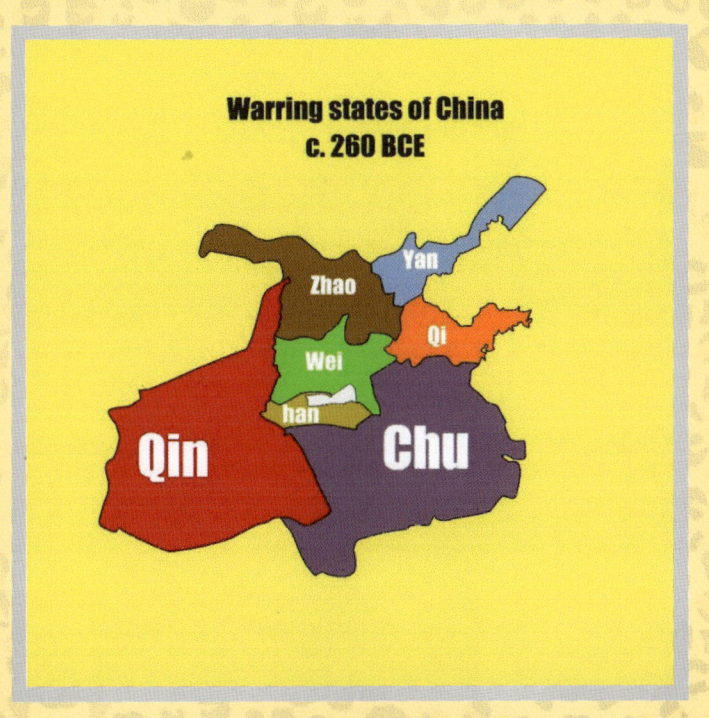

Warring states of China c. 260 BCE

Between 535 and 286 BCE, there was a lot of conflict between the states, and 358 wars took place. That's a crazy number for wars, right? The battle started yet again. The prize that everyone wanted was to be the one ruler of all of China. King Zhao of Qin defeated King Nan of Zhou and conquered West Zhou in 256 BCE. His grandson, King Zhuangxiang of Qin, conquered East Zhou. The Zhou Dynasty had come to an end.

Chapter 5: The Qin Dynasty

The First Imperial Dynasty

The Qin Dynasty was the first empire in China. The empire existed from 221 to 206 BCE, which is not a long time at all. However, it had a great impact on Chinese culture.

The First Emperor of Qin

Qin Shi Huang was the first emperor of Qin, and the dynasty was named after him. Qin had big plans for China. He started to improve his military so that he could seize the five states around Qin. He did this in 221 BCE, and a unified Chinese empire was born.

Qin Shi Huang
https://en.wikipedia.org/wiki/File:Qinshihuang.jpg

A Unified China

Qin Shi Huang was a strong leader who wouldn't stop until he had everyone under his will. He organized 36 command areas on the land and assigned a governor, a military commander, and an imperial inspector to each. They all had to report back to him. He moved important families to the capital, Xianyang, so that he could keep an eye on them. He divided the lands into 36 command areas, each supervised by a governor, a military commander, and an imperial inspector, all of whom reported to him. He truly was ruling over everyone. People's weapons were taken and melted down.

Qin Shi Huang did a lot for the people, too. He made new currency, simplified weights and measurements. This meant that his people could trade using only one currency and use one weight system. This made things a lot easier for everyone. He ordered his men to build wagon axles of a specific size so that they could fit nicely on the roads. It is always better to drive in something that fits on the roads, isn't it?

The Simple Script

The area that Qin Shi Huang conquered was home to many different cultures and languages. So he knew he had to work hard to bring everyone together. He started with a standard written script that all his people could use. The script was simple, so it made it easy for people to write quickly. People liked it because they could keep records faster than ever before. The fantastic thing about the script was that it made it possible for people who didn't speak the same language to communicate using writing. Although he encouraged his people to write, he looked at everything that they wrote. If he didn't like what they wrote, he would burn their work. Imagine your teacher burning your homework. As the years passed, he became more controlling, even sentencing the writer to death if he disagreed with their books.

The Great Wall
Credit: Peter Dowley https://www.flickr.com/photos/pedronet/2639612640

Buildings and Construction

Qin had thousands of men under his command. He divided them into two groups. One group had to defend his land against the tribes of the south. The other group had to build palaces, canals, and roads. Qin wanted to have the largest palace in the world. So he ordered his builders to build the E Pang Palace. They started building it in 212 BCE, but it was so big that they only finished the front of it when he died. So he never saw his precious palace.

He ordered his men to build irrigation systems all over the land. He also wanted to keep his land safe from attacks. So he created 44 small cities surrounded by walls overlooking the river. He was defending a line of 3000 miles. It was a tough project, and many of his workers died. Some died because they got injured, and some died because they were just too tired. This led him to begin the Great Wall of China and the Terracotta Soldiers.

The Secret Life of Qin

Terracotta Army:
Credit: Güldem Üstün https://www.flickr.com/photos/guldem/26279806738

Qin Shi Huang had a stressful life. A sorcerer Lu Sheng warned him of his safety. Qin started traveling through secret tunnels and lived in secret places. His people were not allowed to use his name on any documents. Anyone who shared his location would face their death. He wanted to live forever. He ordered his advisors to find herbs that would make him live forever. Of course, they never did. He was so dedicated to living forever that he ordered his men to make an army of terracotta soldiers to be buried with him when he died. The soldiers were meant to protect him in the afterlife.

End of the Qin Dynasty

Qin Shi Huang died in 210 BCE, and his young son became the new emperor. This didn't go well. Two years later, most of the empire was fighting against the new emperor. Warlord Xiang Yu battled against the Qin army and won. He killed the emperor, destroyed the capital, and divided the empire into 18 states.

Liu Bang was leading the Han River Valley. He battled against other kings and then fought against Xiang Yu for three years. Finally, in 202 BCE Xiang Yu died. Lin Bang became the emperor of the Han Dynasty.

Chapter 6: The Han Dynasty

The Second Imperial Dynasty

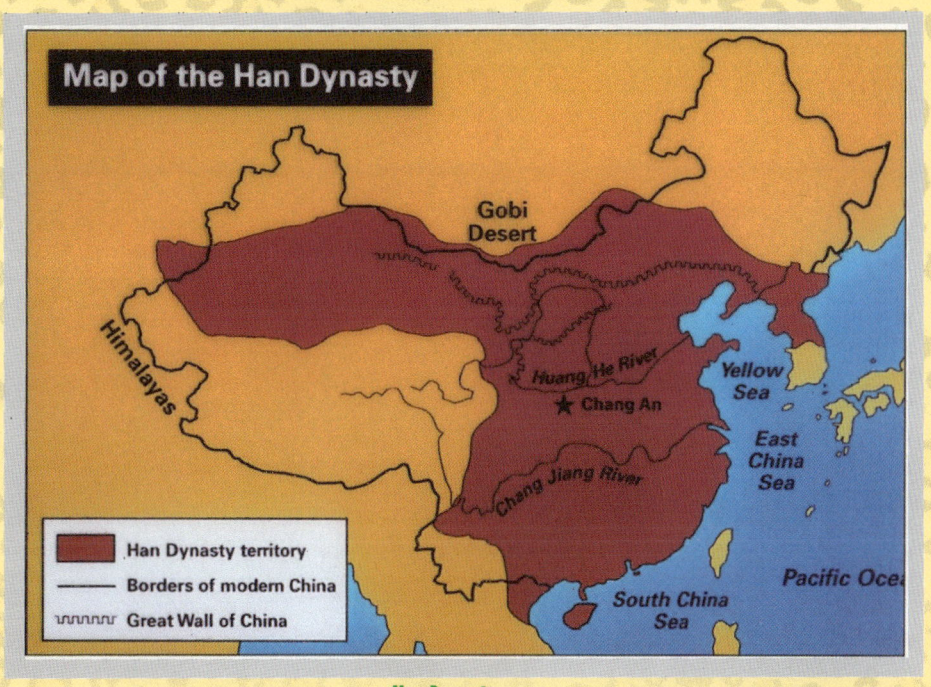

Han Dynasty map
https://www.china-mike.com/wp-content/uploads/2011/01/Han-dynasty-Map.jpg

The second Imperial Dynasty of China was the Han Dynasty. The Han Dynasty ruled China from 206 BCE to 220 AD. The people of Qin were still mourning the death of emperor Qin Sin Huang when warlord Xiang Yu took control for a short time. Finally, it was emperor Liu Bang who took control of the Han Dynasty in 202 BCE.

Western Han

Western Han paper Credit: Gary Todd
https://commons.wikimedia.org/wiki/File:Western_Han_Paper_(10095191884).jpg

Liu Bang established the Han capital of Chang'an. It was along the Wei River. Although most of the Qin Dynasty's palaces have been destroyed, there was one that stood perfectly. Liu Bang moved into the palace and changed his name to Emperor Gaozu. The period of Western Han started and lasted until 23AD.

Han model boat
Credit: David Schroeter https://www.flickr.com/photos/drs2biz/3441662734

Gaozu didn't want any more battles for dominance, so he replaced the kings of the surrounding kingdoms with members of his own family before he died in 195 BCE. The joke was on Gaozu because his family members had plans of their own.

Empress Lu Zhi

After Gaozu died, Empress Lu Zhi tried to take control by killing some of Gaozu's sons. Lu Zhi would stop at nothing to be in complete control. She even killed her mother. The three kings who ruled after Gaozu were puppet kings. Empress Lu Zhi controlled them. She was finally the one with the power. She was so feared that no one would stand up to her. Could you imagine someone so cruel and scary? The struggle went on for 15 years before one of Gaozu's sons, Wan, killed her entire family and became emperor.

Wang Mang and the New Dynasty

In 9AD, the Western Han ended when Wang Mang seized the throne. The last several emperors had died young, and their power had mostly gone to their uncles. Wang broke this tradition by declaring "The New Dynasty."

Wang Mang believed in giving back to the people. Much like a Chinese Robin Hood, he took from the rich and gave to the poor. He took wealthy estates and gave them to the peasants. Everything seemed to go very well for the New Dynasty, but it was just the calm before the storm. In 23 AD, there was a huge flood. The peasants were angry, and they started a group called the

Red Eyebrows. They called themselves the Red Eyebrows because they painted their eyebrows red before battle. This group killed Wang Mang and destroyed Chang'an.

The grandson of Gaozu, Liu Xiu, took over as emperor. He established the Eastern Han Dynasty.

Eastern Han

Emperor Liu Xiu was weak, and the Red Eyebrows killed him within two years of his reign. It was Emperor Guangwu who took control of Eastern Han. He had many plans to prevent the chaos of the Xin Dynasty from happening again. He set firm rules for everyone and moved the capital to Luoyang, where he could keep an eye on it.

The Han Dynasty became strong under the leadership of Guangwu. However, the emperors who followed Guangwu didn't care about the people at all. The third emperor, Huan, is said to have been so lazy that he would arrest anyone who gave him more work. The Eastern Han was weakening because of bad leadership. The people lost faith in the emperors. The Han was trying to expand to Vietnam and Korea. These efforts were costly. People grew even more unhappy when they were forced to pay higher taxes. They began to hate their emperor, and he stood alone.

Emperor Lingdi took over from Huan, and the people struggled with floods and hunger. With the Han at its weakest, Warlord Cao started a war to gain complete control of China. Although he was defeated, the country was divided up into three kingdoms. They were Cao Wei, Eastern Wu, and Shu Han. They each claimed the Mandate of Heaven, and that was the end of the Han Dynasty. The Six Dynasties Period followed the Han, a time that would transform China.

The Legacy of The Han Dynasty

The Han Dynasty was so much more than just years of battles and wars. It was a time where people were learning and growing very much. The dynasty improved their schools so that their people could be educated. The Han Dynasty was also a time where art blossomed. Most of the art came from tombs of important families. We can still see The Wu Family site today. It is two underground chambers under four shrines. The tomb has 70 carved stones, painted ceilings, and walls with paintings of historical people.

Han board game
https://images.metmuseum.org/CRDImages/as/original/DP372026.jpg

The site contained about 3,000 Han Dynasty art figures made of silver, bronze, gold, jade, silk, and pottery.

The Han developed music theory and invented the seismometer - that's a tool used to detect and record earthquakes! It also invented paper and the waterwheel. The people were inspired - improving on the calendar, mathematics, cartography (the drawing and studying of maps), metallurgy (the science of metal), architecture, and astronomy. The Han Dynasty also created the Silk Road, a trade route that created a direct link to the West.

Chapter 7: Inventions, Arts and Trade

The Ancient Chinese were heroes when it came to inventions and technology. Many of these inventions changed the entire world and are still helpful today. This ancient culture made such an impact on our everyday life, that they are thanked for making the Four Great Inventions. These are the inventions that allowed our human race to evolve to where we are today. The four inventions are paper, gunpowder, the compass, and printing. However, China did so much more for us than those four inventions. Let's look at those - and all the other amazing inventions China has given us.

Silk Road landscape
Credit: fdecomite https://www.flickr.com/photos/fdecomite/4367669018

Silk

Traditional Chinese silk Credit: sergeant killjoy
https://www.flickr.com/photos/doc_bosco/2085169813

Silk is a very popular material around the world because it is soft and light. In 138 BCE, Emperor Wu sent a man named Zhang Qian to contact tribes to the west. The Xiongnu tribe captured him and his party, but Zhang Qian escaped and continued west. He reached the area we now know as Afghanistan, which was called Bactria at the time. There, he saw bamboo and Chinese textiles, but he was confused about how they got there. The people of Bactria told him it came from a kingdom called Shendu. In fact, what Zhang Qian didn't know was that silk had been found in Ancient Egypt, Rome, and the whole of Levant (the region along the eastern Mediterranean shores).

Zhang Qian explored the area for 13 years. Then he went back to his emperor. He told the emperor about Shendu and drew maps of how to get there. The maps were used more and more, resulting in the international trade route called Silk Road. Thanks to Zhang Qian, it was now possible for China to trade with Europe.

The Chinese learned how to make silk from the cocoons of silkworms, something they kept secret for hundreds of years. After China has been using silkworms for hundreds of years, Europe also started with the practice. Today silk is available everywhere.

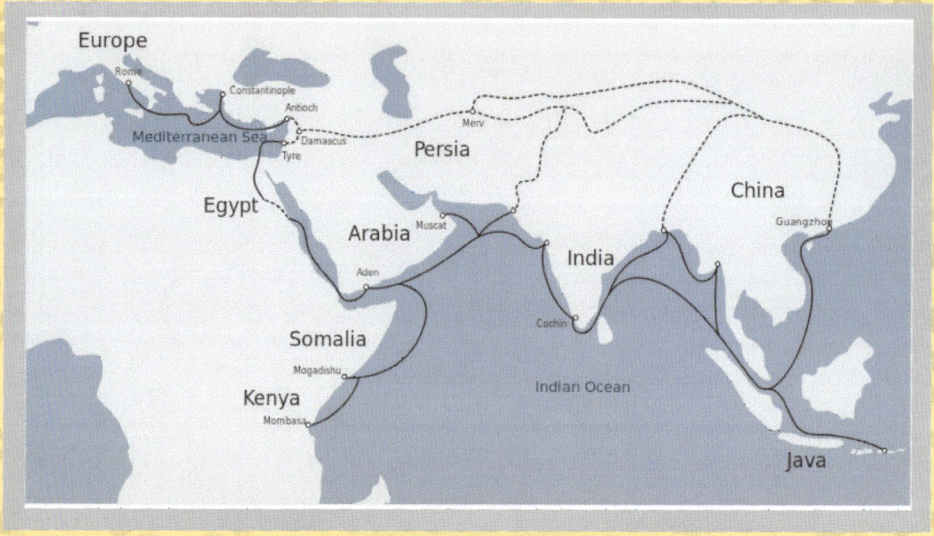

Silk Road map trail
Credit: Belsky https://commons.wikimedia.org/wiki/File:Silk_Road.svg

Paper

The Chinese invented paper and many uses for it. These uses included paper money and playing cards. Can you imagine our lives without those two things? It sure is hard to do. Paper was invented in China during the Han Dynasty by Cai Lun around AD 105.

Ancient Chinese paper
https://commons.wikimedia.org/wiki/File:Fangmatan_paper_map.jpg

This inventor pounded ingredients like bamboo, hemp, rags, fishing nets, and mulberry tree bark into a pulp. Then he mixed it in water and spread it flat. The use of paper spread quickly through the empire, and so began people's love of paper.

Printing

Woodblock printing was invented in AD 868. Images or letters would be carved onto wood blocks, and the ink was applied. Paper would be pressed on the blocks, and the process repeated. More movable printing types were invented about 200 years later. This is *very impressive* since Europe didn't invent the printing press until hundreds of years later. Printing started in the time of the Han Dynasty. People used ink rubbings on paper or cloth from texts on stone tables. If you think about important books and papers have been in history, it's easy to understand why printing is considered as one of the Four Great Inventions of China!

The Compass

Have you ever been lost? It's not a fun experience. The Ancient Chinese didn't like it either. In fact, they disliked it so much that they found a way to avoid it. The Chinese invented the magnetic compass to help find the correct direction. They used this in city planning at first, but it became very important to map makers and ships' navigation.

Gunpowder

Chemists invented gunpowder in the 9th century. It is said that they were trying to find the Elixir of Immortality. Soon after, engineers learned that gunpowder has military uses such as bombs, guns, mines, and even rockets. They also invented fireworks and made great beautiful firework displays for celebrations. We still use fireworks today to celebrate big occasions.

Boat Rudders

It was difficult to steer large ships in Ancient China. The rudder - usually a wood piece that hung down below the water to help guide the boat - was invented to help lead these large ships more quickly. The rudder made it possible for the Chinese to build massive ships in AD 200, years before Europe started building them! Boat rudders are still used today, making it possible to steer large ships that would otherwise be nearly impossible to move.

The Umbrella

We have all had a day where we got stuck in the rain. As our clothes, shoes, and bag got wet, we wished we remembered our umbrella! If you had to guess how long umbrellas have been around, what would you say? If your answer was more than 2 million days, you would be correct. The umbrella was first invented in 3500 BCE by the Chinese. Just like today, the Chinese used umbrellas to keep them from getting soaking wet when it rained. They also used the umbrella to keep them safe from the sun. Remember, they didn't have any sunblock back then! The Ancient Chinese used bamboo and oil-paper to make their umbrellas.

Porcelain

Porcelain is not just something pretty that Grandma puts her Sunday bakes on. It is an invention that changed the future of art around the world. The story of porcelain dates back to Eastern Han. The people heated ceramic materials to a high enough temperature to create porcelain. Porcelain is very durable, and we can still see pieces that they made in Eastern Han on display today. Although the porcelain is older than 2000 years old, it is still very colorful.

The Wheelbarrow

The wheelbarrow was invented in China by a man named Chuk Liang in the first century. He was tired of having too much to carry around. So he created the wheelbarrow to make his chores easier to do. Wheelbarrows make so many people's lives easier, and it is more popular than ever before. The design of the wheelbarrow hasn't changed in 1,700 years. Now, that is amazing.

Iron Casting

About 300 BCE, ironworkers in China discovered that burning iron ore makes a thick metallic liquid mixed with charcoal. This led them to invent cast iron. The hot liquid was poured into a mold that cools into hard, durable cast iron. Cast iron became an important part of Chinese life. The Chinese were making 150,000 tons a year before Europe even started making cast iron.

Hot Air Balloons

Have you ever been in a hot air balloon and wondered how it came to be? During the Three Kingdoms era, China invented the hot air balloon. The Chinese made Kongming lanterns that were lanterns that flew into the air unmanned. They used them to send signals to the military. These lanterns spread across Asia, and you can still see them today during the Loi Krathong Festival in Thailand.

Seismographs

The Chinese invented the first seismograph, or earthquake detector, in AD 132. The ancient seismometer (pronounced "size-mom-metter") was built with a large bronze bowl with eight dragon heads holding bronze balls. During an earthquake, the earth's movement would make a ball fall, showing the direction of the quake. So, hold onto your socks and hat whenever those dragons start dropping balls!

The Kite

About 3,000 years ago, the Chinese invented kites during the Han Dynasty. The first kite was made of silk and wood, and a farmer flew it. He tied a piece of silk to a string and then tied the line to his hat! The Chinese used kites to send messages - since they didn't have smartphones like we do.

Later the Chinese military attached bamboo pipes to their kites. As the kites flew over their enemies, the wind passed through the pipes, causing a whistling sound. The noise caused the troops to panic and run away. Imagine armies of strong men running from a kite! Kites came in many fantastic shapes, sizes, and bright colors. You could find kites shaped like birds, butterflies, tadpoles, and dragons. What kind of kite would you choose?

Matches

Matches are handy tools if you ever go on a camping trip. Did you know that the Chinese were the first people to invent matches? Matches were invented during the kingdom of Northern Ch'i in AD 577. The Chinese used sticks and pine wood to make the first matches. So, don't forget every time you strike a match: you are using a Chinese invention.

The Fishing Rod

An ancient painting showed the existence of the fishing rod in China. The first fishing reel was also invented in China. This was thanks to the Yellow river. The river has always been an inspiration for the people of Ancient China, driving them to get better tools to fish.

Acupuncture

Acupuncture (placing needles into skin to help with pain and illnesses) treatment has been around since 6000 BCE, and people used long and sharp bones to do the treatments. Today's treatments are far less scary. Acupuncture is very useful and has many benefits for the body.

Abacus

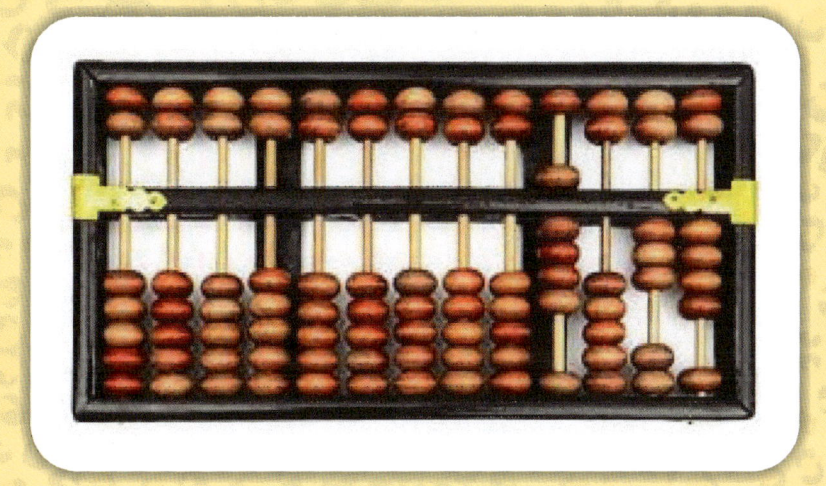

Abacus Credit: Felix Winkelnkemper
https://www.flickr.com/photos/winkelnkemper/47593100081

People in China first made an abacus about 2,500 years ago. An abacus is a very helpful math tool. In a way, it was the first computer that was ever invented. We can still use an abacus today to solve addition, subtraction, and multiplication problems. Many kids see the Abacus as a toy, but it is so much more than that; it has so many benefits!

Let's look at what an Abacus can do for you:
- It can help with concentration
- It can improve your listening and visual skills
- It can give you a better imagination
- It can help your memory improve
- It can help with your speed and accuracy
- It can boost your creativity
- It can increase your self-confidence

That is a long list of benefits. You can still find these in stores, so get yours and start enjoying this Ancient Chinese tool.

The I Ching

There is a book that is known as the world's oldest oracle (a message given by a prophet). It is the I Ching. It has helped people for generations. We can still buy the I Ching today. It is a fantastic collection of pictures, poetry, and advice. The I Ching is very simple to use. All you need is a copy of the book and three coins.

First, you toss the coins and let them fall six times. A "heads" is worth three, while a "tails" is only worth two. After your six attempts, add up the totals. If your total is an even number, draw a broken line (- -). If your total number is odd, draw an unbroken line (—). In the end, you will end up with two sets of three lines. Then, find each of your sets in the book and see what they mean!

Everyone's Favorite Treat: Ice Cream

Imagine our world without ice cream. It's something we don't want to do. Luckily, we don't need to because ice cream was invented in China around 200 BCE. It happened by accident when a mixture of rice and milk was frozen in the snow. Years later, the famous explorer, Marco Polo, saw ice cream while traveling to China. He went back to Italy and told them of the wonderful frozen treat.

Calligraphy

The most important ancient Chinese art form is calligraphy. It was first seen during the Han Dynasty in 206 BCE. People used animal hair - or sometimes a feather - to make brushes that were very flexible. They were then tied to a bamboo handle to make a brush. Writers used soot and animal glue to create a dried cake of ink. People first painted on wood and bamboo. Later (from around 300 BCE), they started painting on silk. After paper was invented around AD 105, people used it for calligraphy, too. Have you ever tried calligraphy?

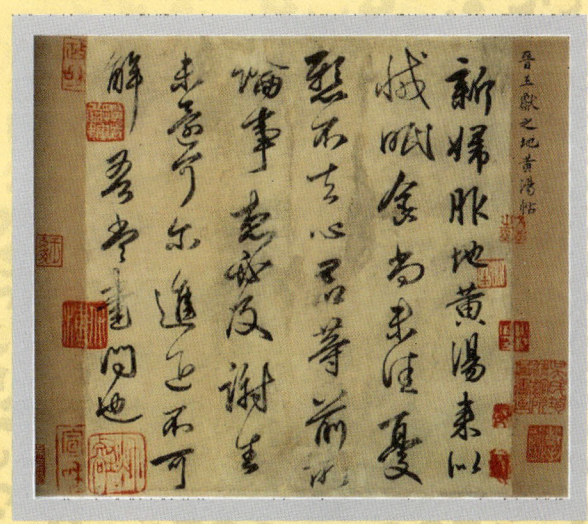

Chinese calligraphy
https://commons.wikimedia.org/wiki/File:Wang_Xianzi_Imitation_by_Tang_Dynasty.JPG

The Suspension Bridge

The Han Dynasty developed the suspension bridge, a flat roadway that is suspended from cables. By AD 90, Han engineers were building simple versions of these structures with wooden planks. Suspension bridges are still used today, and although the materials are improved, the method that the Ancient Chinese used, remains.

Tea

Tea has been very important in China, and it still is today. In fact, legend would suggest that tea had something to do with the story of silk. It is said that silk was discovered when a cocoon fell into a cup of imperial tea from a mulberry bush above.

The discovery of tea itself dates back to 2737 BCE when leaves from an overhanging Camellia bush fell into a cup of water. Emperor Shen Nung drank the tea, and so, the love of tea began.

Lacquer

You might be asking what lacquer is and why it is important. Well, lacquer is a liquid that you can use to protect your wooden furniture and make it shiny. You paint the liquid on wooden surfaces and then you wait for it to dry. If you apply it correctly, it can help your wooden furniture last much longer. It is also repels insects and water, so you can use it on a boat or even an umbrella. Now, that is awesome. Lacquer was first made in the Shang Dynasty.

Ancient China really has improved our lives greatly. Here is what they did for us:

   A - Amazing tools to use everyday

   N - New ways to use paper

   C - Calligraphy and other beautiful ways to write on paper

   I - Ice cream, yes, please!

   E - Exciting ways to fish with the fishing rod and reel

   N - Nice entertainment with kites

   T - The wheelbarrow

   C - Casting of iron

   H - Handy matches to make fire

   I - Interesting ways to do math with an Abacus

   N - Neat ways to see the world by using hot air balloons

   A - A great way to keep dry by using an umbrella

Chapter 8: The Armies of Ancient China

Warfare

Before the warring states of China were united, each state had its own territory and military. After the states became united, an organized army was formed. Although the states were united, emperors still wanted to claim more territory. An army was needed to conquer the surrounding land. For many centuries, China was often attacked by Mongol tribes to the north. China's military had to make sure that Chinese lands were safe! The soldiers worked very hard, and they had a stressful life. If something went wrong, it was their fault. They always had to give their best.

The Army

China was often at war during the Han Dynasty. There were also a lot of attacks from enemies north of the Han Dynasty. China's army was made up of men who served in the military for two years. If it was a peaceful time, the army was sent on missions to get more land for China. That meant that even in peaceful times, there was no rest for soldiers. There was always more land to find and seize.

Soldiers

During the Han Dynasty, all healthy men between the age of 23 and 56 had to serve in the army for two years. If there was an emergency, these men were called back to help *even if their two years were over*. If it was a peaceful time, the men who were still busy in their two years became guards. They had to stand at different points along the walls of cities and keep them safe.

Soldiers were not paid with money for their help; instead, they were paid with *food*. They had to wear their full uniform at all times. How hard would you work for a meal? These soldiers had no choice other than to work hard!

Weapons

The early armies in China used chariots and bronze weapons to fight. In the later years, as they got better at making weapons, they used iron weapons, too. The weapons were bows, arrows, and swords. Later they developed the crossbow, and people stopped using chariots. Crossbows were very helpful in battle. They could break the enemy's armor and travel 200 meters! So, it became one of the most important weapon in Ancient China. Crossbows became so useful that they were included in the burial tomb of Emperor Qin.

Ancient Chinese weapons Credit: Gary Todd
https://commons.wikimedia.org/wiki/File:Eighteen_Weapons_of_Ancient_China_(9883592815).jpg

Armor

Leather and metal were mostly used to make armor. To create strong armor, metal and leather pieces were stitched over each other and then stitched to cloth. Soldiers could still move around and be protected. The Han Dynasty introduced helmets as part of armor. Helmets improved the chances of soldiers surviving battles.

Han iron scale armor replica
https://www.flickr.com/photos/101561334@N08/9873767864

Defense

Enemy tribes often attacked China, and the army had to defend their land. Some of the tribes trained their soldiers from a very young age, teaching them to fight and ride horses very well. Still, the army had a lot of soldiers who didn't fight well; they were just doing their two years of service.

Many of these attacks were hard, and China lost a lot of soldiers. It isn't really fair to let someone who just joined the army fight against someone who has been fighting since he was a small boy. But that was life in Ancient China.

Sun Tze and The Art of War

A famous Chinese general, Sun Tzu, wrote a very important book called The Art of War, and it was written 2,400 years ago! The book has 13 chapters, and it taught readers step-by-step ideas of how to win a war.

Sun Tzu statue Credit: 663highland
https://commons.wikimedia.org/wiki/File:Enchoen27n3200.jpg

Sun Tzu means *Master Sun*, and he lived during the Spring and Autumn Period - from about 771 to 476 BCE. His family members were in the army, so he learned a lot about the battle as a boy. When he was a young man, he became an advisor to the warlord of the state of Wu, helping the warlord defeat his enemies. It is said that he wrote The Art of War on bamboo strips! Isn't it amazing how much writing has changed since then? Imagine reading your science textbook on bamboo?

The Heavenly horses

There were many different kinds of horses in Ancient China. The horses in South China were small and light. The horses in North China were big and strong.

The Heavenly Horses of Ancient China were very different. The horses were tall with a small head and a long neck. They had a long back with narrow bodies. Their legs were long. Their mane was thin. The thing that stood out about these horses was their sweat; it looked red, making people think of blood. This made them very popular in battle, because the red sweat scared the enemy.

The Terracotta Army

The first emperor of China, Emperor Qin Shi Huang, had a huge tomb for his burial. This was the Terracotta Army and there were more than 8,000 life size statues of soldiers buried with the emperor. The reason for this very full tomb was that Emperor Qin wanted to live forever. He always tried to find the true answer for living forever, the real "elixir of life". Eternal life wasn't the only thing he spent time and resources on. He also spent a lot of resources and time on building his own tomb. It was the largest single tomb that any leader in the world has ever had! Why did he want to share his final resting place with more than 8,000 terracotta soldiers?

He thought a massive army would keep him safe and help him be powerful in the afterlife. He died more than 2000 years ago in 210 BCE. We can still see the terracotta army today.

What do the soldiers look like?

The soldiers are life-size statues, and they are around 5 feet 11 inches tall. Some soldiers were as tall as b 6 foot 7 inches! Even though there as literally thousands of them, no two are alike. Isn't that amazing?

The soldiers are all of different ages. They have different hairstyles, and faces. They even have different facial expressions.

Some of them are angry, some are calm, and some seem ready for battle.

They also have different clothing and armor, but some have no armor at all. It is thought that the soldiers without armor might have been spies. These soldiers still impress us today, but imagine how impressive they must have been 2000 years ago! They were painted to look even more realistic. They were also covered with a special finish, called a *lacquer finish*.

They held onto real weapons - crossbows, daggers, maces, spears, and swords - which were the most used at that time. Emperor Qin took his afterlife power so seriously that he used real weapons in his terracotta army instead of giving them to his soldiers. So, they had to make more weapons for actual battle.

Terracotta soldier
Credit: shankar s. https://www.flickr.com/photos/shankaronline/35557414921

How did they build so many soldiers?

Can you imagine how long and how many people it took to build an army of 8,000 life-size statues? It has been estimated by archeologists that over 700,000 craftsmen worked on the project for many years. The bodies of the soldiers were made in an assembly line. There were molds for making the legs, arms, torsos, and heads. These pieces were then put together and then custom features such as ears, mustaches, hair, and weapons were added at a later time.

There are ten different head shapes for the soldiers. These different head shapes represent people from different areas of China - even with different personalities. The heads were made from customized molds, and as the last step, they were attached to the bodies. It is incredible to see more than 8,000 statues - each with a unique look.

Other statues

Emperor Qin Shi Huang's tomb is most famous for its terracotta soldiers, but there were several other statues that would keep Emperor Qin company in the afterlife. These other statues included 150 life-size cavalry horses and 130 chariots with 520 horses. These statues were buried with the army. Other figures have been found in other areas of the tomb. They are thought to be government officials and entertainers.

Han cavalry
https://commons.wikimedia.org/wiki/File:Dahuting_Tomb_mural,_cavalry_and_chariots,_Eastern_Han_Dynasty.jpg

Farmers discovered the Terracotta Army while they were digging a well in 1974 - more than 2,000 years after the burial of Emperor Qin! The emperor's tomb was located about a mile from where his army was stationed.

The Great Wall of China

The Great Wall of China is an ancient wall - and probably China's most famous feature. Parts of the wall were started in the 7th century BCE, but not entirely completed until the early 1900s by the Qing dynasty. It is made of cement, rocks, bricks, and powdered dirt. It was meant to protect the north from enemy attacks. It is the longest structure ever built by humans.

How long is the Great Wall of China? It is 13,171 miles 13,171 miles long. It is 30 feet wide, and it is 50 feet high. Sections of the wall started before the Ming Dynasty were made with stone and dirt that had been compacted. Later, bricks were used. The wall is incredible, with 7,000 watch towers, block houses for soldiers, and beacons for sending smoke signals.

Chapter 9: Chinese Philosophy and Religions

Lao Tzu

Lao Tzu, who is also called Laozi or Lao Tze, was the head figure of Taoism – a spiritual practice. Some people say Lao Tze was a record-keeper in the court during the Zhou Dynasty. Other people say that is not true, and that he is just a myth. Some legends tell us that Lao Tzu was born as an old man with long earlobes who lived to be 990 years old. What do you think?

The legend tells us that Lao Tze was tired of working in the court, so he left and rode on a water buffalo to the western border of the Chinese empire. He was dressed as a farmer, but the guard at the border recognized him and asked him to write down his wisdom. Lao Tze wrote words that were so incredible that they became a sacred text

Lao Tzu
https://commons.wikimedia.org/wiki/File:Lao_Tzu_-_Project_Gutenberg_eText_15250.jpg

called the <u>Tao Te Ching</u>. It is said that he was never seen again. Stories about Lao Tzu have been passed down through different Chinese philosophical schools for over two thousand years.

Today, at least twenty million Taoists live around the world, especially in China and Taiwan. They practice meditation, chant sacred texts, and worship various gods and goddesses in temples run by priests. Taoists also make pilgrimages to five sacred mountains in Eastern China to pray at the temples and absorb spiritual energy from these holy places, which are believed to be cared for by immortals.

Taoist temple

Confucius

Confucius
https://commons.wikimedia.org/wiki/File:Confucius_statue_in_beijing_(cropped).jpg

Confucius, whose Chinese name was Kong Fu Zi, was born in 551 BCE in the Zhou Dynasty, on east coast of China. He was born to a "shi" class family.

The shi were middle-class people - not rich, not poor. They were not noble people, but they had more money than the common people.

He traveled between different states and advised governors who were at war. He believed people should be given opportunities - or chances to get more powerful or wealthy - based on their talents and not on what family they were born into.

He started his life as a shepherd before working in the government of his small town. He eventually became a top advisor to the local authorities.

Confucius proved his idea of being rewarded due to your talents (not your family) worked because he worked hard to create his own life.

Confucius spent his time learning and traveling. People started to notice him, and they wanted him to teach their sons. So, Confucius became the first private teacher in China. Before he was the first teacher, sons were taught by their families.

After a lot of studying and learning from different people, Confucius wrote a set of ideas called *Confucianis*. This was not a religion, but a *way of life*. It is a philosophy that can help people be their best; a set of rules that help people care more for others and be more responsible.

Confucianism's main ideas are:

- Always respect your elders
- Always be polite and gracious to other people
- It is important to learn, always
- Be a person with good morals
- Be kind, honest and loyal Be loyal, honest and kind
- Don't overdo things

It was only after his death that Confucianism became popular.

Buddhism

There are many forms of Buddhism around the world with Chinese Buddhism being one of the oldest forms. Chinese Buddhists believe in a combination of Taoism and Mahayana Buddhism. Yes, big words! Taoism is based on being humble and doing your religious duty. Mahayana Buddhism is more concerned with doing good for others, and everyone becoming "enlightened."

The Laughing Buddha is the most famous picture of the Buddha in China. Chinese Buddhism is different from original Buddhism because, in Chinese Buddhism, Buddha isn't just a teacher; he is a god, and his people should pray for his help.

Chinese Buddhists believe in a mix of Taoism and Buddhism. They pray to Buddha and Taoist gods. But, like Taoists, Chinese Buddhists also pray to their ancestors, thinking they need and want their help.

Chinese Buddhism is different in another way: how they picture Buddha. In the original Buddhist teachings, Buddha is very thin because he was always fasting (going without food). However, in Chinese Buddhism, the Laughing Buddha (or Budai) is shown as being fat and laughing. This is because the main goal of Chinese Buddhists is *to be happy*.

Chapter 10: Customs and Festivities

Dragon Boat Festival

A colorful festival was started during the Zhou Dynasty: The Dragon Boat Festival. Every year on the fifth day of the fifth lunar month of the Chinese calendar, the Dragon Boat Festival is celebrated.

The festival serves as a reminder of an Ancient Chinese poet, Qu Yuan, who jumped into a river and died; many believe he did it on purpose.

During the Dragon Boat Festival, traditions are eating rice dumplings, wearing perfume to protect people from evil beings, and exciting, colorful dragon boat racing. People enjoy making their own rice dumplings. They use banana leaves to cover a triangle-shaped rice ball with meat in the middle. Small sachets that smell sweet are given as presents.

Night of Sevens Festival

The Night of Sevens Festival was first celebrated during the Han Dynasty. It takes place on the seventh day of the seventh lunar month. It marks the love between two people.

A couple finds each other again after the Queen of Heaven separated them. One of the traditions during the festival is praying for a good husband. People also pray to the stars during the Night of the Sevens Festival.

Moon Festival

The Moon Festival is also known as the Mid-Autumn Festival. It started during the Zhou Dynasty, and happens in September. It is a celebration of the harvest.

Traditions during the festival are eating moon cakes - something that began under the Yuan Dynasty. Moon cakes are small round cakes, usually made with a buttery pastry and stuffed with a soft filling. They can be pressed into special molds to have pretty shapes, or stamped with a special message.

Have you ever had a moon cake? There are moon cakes and sun cakes available today. Moon cakes are the more traditional cakes with one filling on the inside. Sun cakes are baked with an egg yolk in the middle of

Mid-Autumn Festival
Credit: Shizhao https://commons.wikimedia.org/wiki/File:Mid-Autumn_Festival-beijing.jpg

the cake, so when you bite into it, it looks like you are staring into the sun. Yum! Moon Festival is celebrated by having a big barbeque outside. Everyone celebrates happily as they eat together.

Double Ninth Festival

The number nine was very lucky in Ancient China. It was a good number for dragons and emperors. Therefore, on the ninth day of the ninth lunar month (usually in October), the Double Ninth Festival is celebrated.

Traditions on this day are drinking chrysanthemum tea. The tea is supposed to protect people from evil spirits. People also climb a hill or mountain.

Winter Solstice Festival

The shortest day of the year is celebrated with the Winter Solstice Festival. This celebration started during the Han Dynasty.

Traditions on this day are sacrificing to the ancestors. People have no work on the day; instead they can enjoy their day with family and friends.

Chinese New Year

This celebration is just as important today as it was in Ancient China. It is also celebrated the same way. In Ancient China, people would welcome the beginning of the New Year by setting off firecrackers. Back then, the firecrackers were made with gunpowder and bamboo.

Traditions of the celebration are making dishes with pork, chicken, and lamb. It is meant to make the land fertile for the year ahead. In Ancient China, people would hang sheep and chicken skins outside their homes, and burn incense. Today a very important part of the celebration is giving and receiving red envelopes. These envelopes contain money, and they are given to and by family members on New Year's Eve. People have a big New Year's Eve meal and then they play Mahjong (a popular Chinese game played with tiles) for hours. People like to give small oranges as gifts to family and friends because they are meant to bring good luck.

Chinese New Year festive costume
Credit: Dom Crossley https://www.flickr.com/photos/flashcurd/8499214042

The Lantern Festival

Red Lanterns
https://commons.wikimedia.org/wiki/File:Red_lanterns_in_Taichung_Park.jpg

The Lantern Festival was another important festival and is celebrated as a part of the New Year's celebration. The festival celebrates the full moon's light. It is celebrated on the 15th day of the first lunar month (between December and January).

Traditions of the festival include people holding feasts, dancing, and playing games near ponds, streams, and lakes. Sometimes people would float large lanterns on the water.

Richer people celebrated with more likable lamps. However, the emperor had an enormous light. So everyone spent all the money and material to make sure they will have a lucky year ahead.

The Chinese Calendar

The Chinese calendar has been used for thousands of years. It is still used today to mark traditional Chinese holidays.

The Chinese calendar was made by many of the Chinese dynasties of Ancient China.

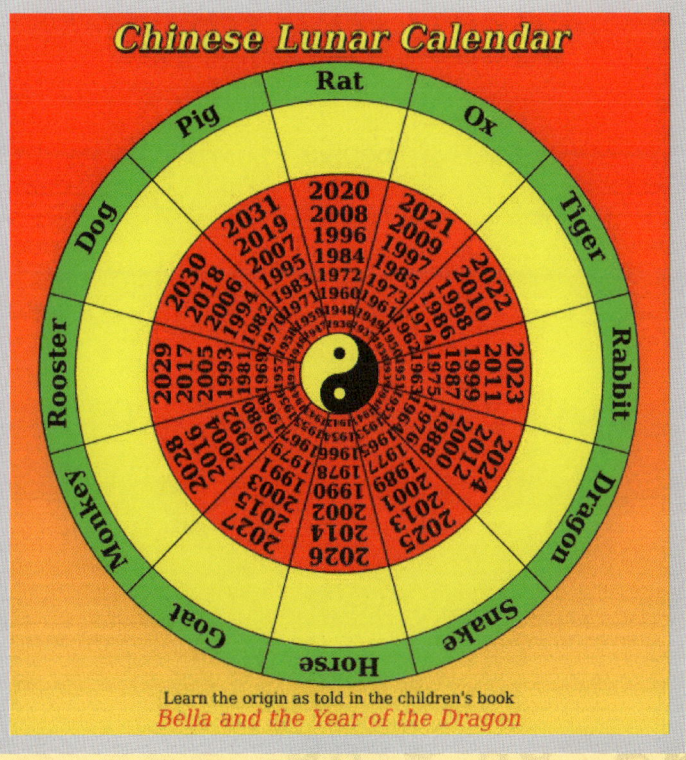

Chinese Calendar
https://freesvg.org/chinese-lunar-calendar-1

However, in 104 BCE, during Emperor Wu's rule of the Han Dynasty, the calendar we use today was created. This calendar is included the days, weeks, and months of a particular year, and was called the Tai Chu calendar.

Every year in the Chinese calendar is named after an animal. Twelve animals repeat in a cycle, so, every twelve years, the cycle repeats itself. It was believed that people had the same personalities as the animal of their birth year.

Let's look at the animals and what they mean.

Year of the Rat

Years: 1960, 1972, 1984, 1996, 2008, 2020

Personality of the rat: charming, loyal, and funny

Who do people who were born in the year of the rat get along with? They get along with people who were born in the year of the dragon and monkey. They do not get along with people who were born in the year of the horse.

Year of the Ox

Years: 1961, 1973, 1985, 1997, 2009, 2021

Personality of the ox: hardworking, serious, patient, and trustworthy

Who do people who were born in the year of the ox get along with? They get along with people who were born in the year of the snake and rooster. They do not get along with people who were born in the year of the sheep.

Year of the Tiger

Years: 1962, 1974, 1986, 1998, 2010

Personality of the tiger: aggressive, brave, ambitious, and intense

Who do people who were born in the year of the tiger get along with? They get along with people who were born in the year of the dog and horse. They do not get along with people who were born in the year of the monkey.

Year of the Rabbit

Years: 1963, 1975, 1987, 1999, 2011

Personality of the rabbit: popular, lucky, kind, and sensitive

Who do people who were born in the year of the rabbit get along with? They get along with people who were born in the year of the pig and sheep. They do not get along with people who were born in the year of the rooster.

Year of the Dragon

Years: 1964, 1976, 1988, 2000, 2012

Personality of the dragon: energetic, healthy and are lucky with the gift of good fortune and good luck

Who do people who were born in the year of the dragon get along with? They get along with people who were born in the year of the monkey and rat. They do not get along with people who were born in the year of the dog.

Year of the Snake

Years: 1965, 1977, 1989, 2001, 2013

Personality of the snake: smart, jealous, and generous

Who do people who were born in the year of the snake get along with? They get along with people who were born in the year of the rooster and ox. They do not get along with people who were born in the year of the pig.

Year of the Horse

Years: 1966, 1978, 1990, 2002

Personality of the horse: like to travel, attractive, impatient, and popular

Who do people who were born in the year of the horse get along with? They get along with people who were born in the year of the tiger and dog. They do not get along with people who were born in the year of the rat.

Year of the Sheep

Years: 1967, 1979, 1991, 2003

Personality of the sheep or goat: creative, shy, and unsure

Who do people who were born in the year of the sheep get along with? They get along with people who were born in the year of the rabbit and pig. They do not get along with people who were born in the year of the ox.

Year of the Monkey

Years: 1968, 1980, 1992, 2004

Personality of the monkey: curious, naughty, and clever

Who do people who were born in the year of the monkey get along with? They get along with people who were born in the year of the dragon and rat. They do not get along with people who were born in the year of the tiger.

Year of the Rooster

Years: 1969, 1981, 1993, 2005

Personality of the rooster: honest, neat, practical, and proud

Who do people who were born in the year of the rooster get along with? They get along with people who were born in the year of the snake and ox. They do not get along with people who were born in the year of the rabbit.

Year of the Dog

Years: 1958, 1970, 1982, 1994, 2006

Personality of the dog: loyal, honest, sensitive, and moody

Who do people who were born in the year of the dog get along with? They get along with people who were born in the year of the tiger and horse. They do not get along with people who were born in the year of the dragon.

Year of the Pig

Years: 1959, 1971, 1983, 1995, 2007

Personality of the pig: intelligent, sincere, perfectionistic, and noble

Who do people who were born in the year of the pig get along with? They get along with people who were born in the year of the rabbit and sheep. They do not get along with people who were born in the year of the pig.

Could you find your birth year? Do you share the personality traits of your birth year animal?

The great race that led to the Chinese Zodiac Calendar

Years ago, the Jade emperor wanted to measure time for his birthday. He told all the animals that if they could swim across the river, there would be a month of the zodiac calendar named after them.

All the animals lined up excitedly. It was only Rat and Cat that were nervous because they are not good swimmers. They asked Ox if they could sit on his back while he swam; he said it would be ok.

The race started and Rat and Cat sat on Ox's back while he swam. Ox was a strong swimmer, so Rat and Cat were happy. However, when they got close to the end of the race, Rat pushed Cat into the water. Then Rat jumped off of Ox's head and won the race.

Rat had tricked Ox. Ox came second and would forever be after Rat in the Zodiac calendar.

The Jade emperor saw that Rat won and he celebrated. "Well done, Rat," he said, "You are first on the Chinese Zodiac calendar."

What a sneaky and smart Rat!

Plus, if you want to learn more about tons of other exciting historical periods, check out our other books!

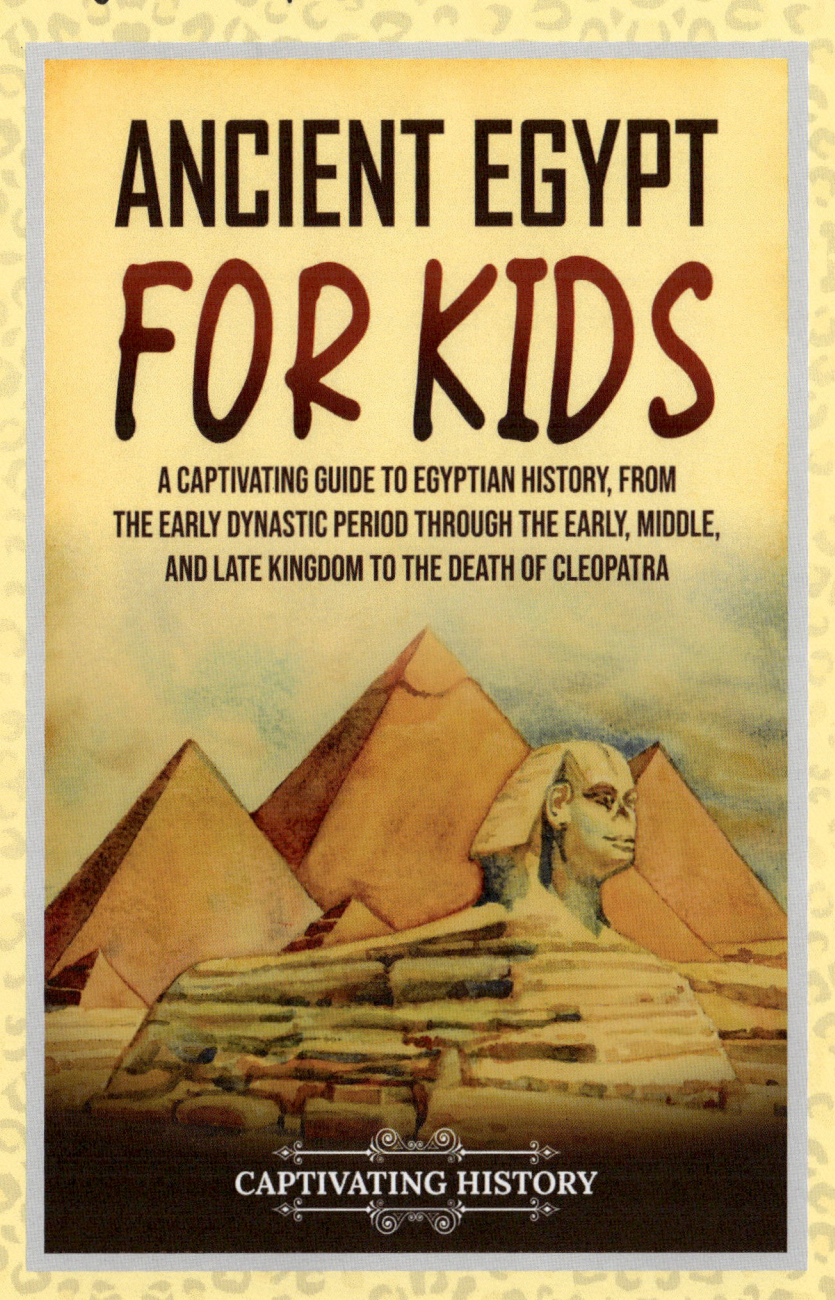

ANCIENT EGYPT FOR KIDS

A CAPTIVATING GUIDE TO EGYPTIAN HISTORY, FROM THE EARLY DYNASTIC PERIOD THROUGH THE EARLY, MIDDLE, AND LATE KINGDOM TO THE DEATH OF CLEOPATRA

CAPTIVATING HISTORY

BIBLIOGRAPHY

Books:

Ancient Civilizations: The Illustrated Guide to Belief, Mythology, and Art. Professor Greg Wolf, 2005

Ancient China by Dale Anderson, 2005.

Exploring Ancient China by Elaine Landau, 2005.

Celebrate Chinese New Year: With Fireworks, Dragons, and Lanterns by Carolyn Otto, 2009

Websites:

https://www.ducksters.com/history/china/ancient_china.php

https://www.dkfindout.com/us/history/ancient-china/

https://www.historyforkids.net/history-of-china.html

https://kids.nationalgeographic.com/pages/article/chinese-horoscopes